BARON MUNCHAUSEN's

NARRATIVE

OF HIS

MARVELLOUS TRAVELS, &c.

[Price ONE SHILLING.]

ARON MUNCHAUSEN's

NARRATIVE

OF HIS

MARVELLOUS TRAVELS

AND

CAMPAIGNS

IN

RUSSIA.

HUMBLY DEDICATED AND RECOMMENDED

TO

COUNTRY GENTLEMEN;

AND, IF THEY PLEASE,

TO BE REPEATED AS THEIR OWN, AFTER A HUNT,
AT HORSE RACES, IN WATERING-PLACES, AND
OTHER SUCH POLITE ASSEMBLIES; ROUND THE
BOTTLE AND FIRE-SIDE.

OXFORD:

Printed for the EDITOR, and fold by the Bookfellers there and
at Cambridge, alfo in London by the Bookfellers of Picca-
dilly, the Royal Exchange and M. SMITH, at No. 46, in
Fleet-ftreet.

MDCCLXXXVI.
[PRICE ONE-SHILLING.]

E R R A T A.

Page 12, Line 6, for, *my readers;* read *you Gentlemen*
——————— 9, — *them,* read *you.*
—— 13, —— 1, — *their,* read *yours.*
——————— 3, — *they,* read *you.*
—— 40, —— 6, — *miftery,* read *myftery.*

---

††† *The Baron is fuppofed to relate thefe extraordinary Adventures over his Bottle, when furrounded by his Friends.*

PREFACE

BARON MUNNIKHOU-
SON, or MUNCHAU-
SEN, of Bodenweder, near
Hameln on the Weſer, belongs
to the noble family of that
name, which gave to the king's
German dominions the late
prime miniſter, and ſeveral
other public characters, equally
right and illuſtrious. He is

a man

a man of great original humour; and having found that prejudiced minds cannot be reasoned into common sense, and that bold assertors are very apt to bully and speak their audience out of it; he never argues with either of them, but adroitly turns the conversation upon indifferent topicks, and then tells a story of his travels, campaigns, and sporting adventures, in a manner peculiar to himself, and well calculated to awaken and shame the

the common fenfe of thofe who have loft fight of it by prejudice or habit.

As this method has been often attended with good fuccefs, we beg leave to lay fome of his ftories before the Public, and humbly requeft thofe who fhall find them rather extravagant and bordering upon the marvellous, which will require but a very moderate fhare of common fenfe, to exercife the fame upon every

occurrence

occurrence of life, and chiefly upon our Englifh politicks, in which *old habits* and *bold affer-tions*, fet off *by eloquent fpeeches*, and fupported by *conftitutional mobs*, *affociations*, *volunteers*, and *foreign influence*, have of late, we appprehend, but too fuccefsfully turned our brains, and made us the laughing-ftock of Europe, and of France, and Holland in particular.

BARON

BARON MUNCHAUSEN's

NARRATIVE, &c.

I Set off from home on my journey to Ruſſia, in the midſt of
winter, from a juſt notion that
froſt and ſnow muſt of courſe mend
the roads, which every traveller
had deſcribed, as uncommonly bad

through

through the northern parts of Germany, Poland, Courland, and Livonia. I went on horfeback, which, provided mare and rider are in order, is the moft convenient manner of travelling. I was but lightly cloathed, of this, I felt the inconvenience, the more I advanced north-eaft. What muft not a poor old man have fuffered in that fevere weather and climate, whom I faw on a bleak common, in Poland, lying on the road, helplefs, fhivering, and hardly having wherewithall to cover his nakednefs.

I pitied the poor foul. Though I felt exceedingly cold myfelf, I

threw

threw my mantle over him and immediately I heard a voice from the
heavens, bleffing me for that piece
of charity, faying,

"I'll be damned my fon if I do
"not reward it in time."

I went on: night and darkneſs
overtook me. No village was to
be feen. The country was covered
with fnow, and I was unacquaint-
ed with the roads.

Tired I alighted at laſt, and faſh-
oned my horſe to fomething of a
pointed ſtump of a tree, which appeared above the fnow. For the
fake of fafety I took my piftols un-

der

der my arm, and lay down in the snow, not far off, where I slept so soundly, that I did not open my eyes till it was full day light. Great was my aſtoniſhment now, to find myſelf in the midſt of a village, lying in the church-yard. Nor was my horſe to be ſeen, but I heard him ſoon after neigh, ſomewhere above me. On looking upwards I beheld him tied and hanging to the weather-cock of the ſteeple. Matters were now very plain to me: The village had been covered with ſnow that night; a ſudden change of weather had taken place; I had ſunk down to the church-yard whilſt aſleep, gently, and in the ſame fame proportion as the fnow had melted away, and what in the dark I had taken to be a ftump of a little tree appearing above the fnow, to which I had tied my horfe, proved to have been the crofs or weather-cock of the fteeple.

Without long confideration I took one of my piftols, fhot off the halter, brought down the horfe and proceeded on my journey.

He carried me well—yet advancing into Ruffia, where travelling on horfeback is rather unfafhionable in winter, I fubmitted, as I always do, to the cuftom of the country,

took

took a single horse sledge, and drove briskly on towards St. Petersburgh. I do not exactly recollect whether it was in Esthland or Jugemanland, but I remember that in the midst of a dreary forest, somewhere thereabouts, I spied a terrible wolf making after me, with all the speed of ravenous winter hunger. He soon overtook me. There was no possibility of escape. Mechanically I laid myself down flat in the sledge, and let my horse run for our safety. What I apprehended, and hardly hoped or expected happened immediately after. The wolf did not mind me in the least, but took a leap over me, and falling furiously

on

on the horfe, begun inftantly to
tear and devour the hind part of the
poor animal, which ran the fafter
for his pain and terror. Thus un-
noticed and fafe myfelf, I lifted my
head flily up, and with horror I beheld that the wolf ate and broke
his way into the horfe's body. It
was not long before he had fairly
forced himfelf into it; then I took
my advantage, fell upon him with
the but end of my whip. This un-
expected attack in his rear frightened him much; he leaped forward
with all his might; the horfe's car-
cafe dropt to the ground; but in his
place the wolf was in the harnefs,
and I, on my part whipping him
continually

continually, we both arrived, in
full career, fafe at St. Peterfburgh,
contrary to our refpective expecta-
tions, and very much to the afton-
ifhment of the beholders.

I fhall not tire my Readers
with the politicks, arts, fciences,
and hiftory of this magnificent me-
tropolis of Ruffia ; nor trouble them
with the various intrigues, and
pleafing adventures I had in the
politer circles of that country,
where the lady of the houfe always
receives the vifitor with a dram
and a falute. I fhall confine myfelf rather to the greater and nobler
objects

objects of their attention, to horfes
and dogs, of which I have always
been as fond as they are, to foxes,
wolves and bears, of which and
other game Ruffia abounds more
than any other part of the world,
and to fuch fport, manly exercifes,
and feats of gallantry and activity
as make and fhow the gentleman,
better than mufty Greek or Latin,
or all the perfume, finery and ca-
pers of French wits or hair dreffers.

It was fome time before I could
obtain my commiffion in the army,
and for feveral months I was perfectly at liberty to fport away my
time and money in the moft Gen-
tleman-like

tleman-like manner. You may
eaſily imagine, that I ſpent much
of both, out of town, with ſuch
gallant fellows, as knew how to
make the moſt of an open uninncloſed
foreſt country. It is a pleaſing
remembrance, both for the variety
of ſport it afforded, and for the
remarkable ſucceſs I met with in
purſuit of the ſame.

One morning I ſaw through the
windows of my bed-room, that a
large pond, not far off, was, as it
were, covered with wild ducks. In
an inſtant I took my gun from the
corner, run down ſtairs, and out in
ſuch a hurry, that imprudently I
ſtruck

ſtruck my face againſt the door poſt. Fire, light, and ſparks, flew out of my eyes, but it did not prevent my intention. I ſoon came within ſhot, when leveling my piece, I obſerved to my ſorrow, that even the flint had ſprung from the cock, by the violence of the ſhock I had juſt received. There was no time to be loſt. I preſently remembered the effect it had had upon my eyes, therefore opened the pan, leveled my piece againſt the wild fowls, and my fiſt againſt one of my eyes. A hearty blow drew ſparks again, the ſhot went off, and I had five brace of ducks, four widgeons and a couple of teals.

teals. Prefence of mind is the foul of manly exercifes. If foldiers and failors owe to it many of their lucky efcapes, hunters and fportfmen are not lefs beholden to it for many of their fuccefïes. In a noble foreft party in Ruffia, I met a fine black fox, whofe valuable fkin it would have been a pity to tear by ball or fhot. Reynard ftood clofe to a tree. In a twinkling I took out my ball, and placed a good fpike nail in its room, fired and hit him fo cleverly, that I nailed his brufh faft to the tree. I now went up to him, took out my hanger, gave him a crofs cut over the face, laid hold of my whip and fairly flogged him out of

his

his fine fkin, a pleafure and wonder to behold!

Chance and good luck often correct our miftakes: of this I had a fingular inftance foon after, when in the depth of a foreft I faw a wild pig and fow running clofe behind each other. My ball had miffed them, yet the foremoft pig only run away, and the fow ftood motionlefs as fixed to the ground. On examining into the matter I found the latter one to be an old fow, blind with age, which had taken hold of her pig's tail, in order to be led along by filial duty. My ball having paffed between the two,

C   had

had cut this leading ſtring, of which
the old ſow was ſtill chewing the
remainder; and as her former guide
did not draw her on any longer, ſhe
had ſtopt of courſe; I therefore
laid hold of the remaining end of
the pig's tail, and led the old beaſt
home without any further trouble
on my part, and without any re-
luctance or apprehenſion on the part
of the helpleſs old animal.

Terrible theſe wild ſows are,
but more fierce and dangerous are
the boars, one of which I had once
the misfortune to meet in a foreſt
unprepared for attack or defence.
I retired behind an oak tree, juſt
when

when the furious animal levelled a
fide cut at me, with such force,
that his tufks pierced through the
tree, by which means he could neither repeat the blow or retire.——
Ho! ho! thought I, I fhall foon
have you now——fure enough,
——and immediately I laid hold
of a ftone, wherewith I ham-
mered and bent his tufks in fuch a
manner that he could not retreat at
all, and muft wait my return from
the next village, whither I went for
ropes and a cart, to fecure him pro-
perly, and to carry him off fafe and
alive, which perfectly fucceeded.

C 2 You

Your have heard, I dare say, of
the hunters and fportfman's faint
and protector, Saint Hubert; and
of the noble ftag, which appeared
to him in the foreft, with the holy
crofs between his antles. I have
paid my homages to that faint every
year in good fellowfhip, and
feen this ftag a thoufand times,
either painted in churches or em-
broidered in the ftars of his
knights; fo that upon honour and
confcience of a good fportfman, I
hardly know whether there may
not have been formerly, or whether
there are not fuch croffed ftags even
at this prefent day. But let me rather tell what I have feen myfelf.

Having

Having one day spent all my shot, I found myself unexpectedly in presence of a stately stag, looking at me so unconcernedly, as if he had known of my empty pouches. I charged immediately with powder, and upon it a good handful of cherries, of which I had partly sucked the flesh as far as the hurry would permit. Thus I let fly at him, and hit him just on the middle of the forehead, between his antlers. It stunned him—he staggered—yet he made off. A year or two after I was with a party in the same forest—and behold a noble stag comes out with a fine full-grown cherry-tree between his ant-

C 3   lers.

lers. I recollected my former adventure; looked upon him as my property; and brought him to the ground by one shot, which at once gave me the haunce and cherry-sauce; for the tree was covered with the richest fruit, the like I never had tasted before. Who knows but some passionate holy sportsman, or sporting abbot or bishop, may have shot, planted and fixed the cross between the antlers of Saint Hubert's stag in a manner similar to this? They always have been and still are famous for plantations of crosses and antlers; and, in a case of distress or dilemma, which too often happens to gallant

sportsmen,

fportfmen, one is apt to grafp at any thing for fafety, and to try any expedient, rather than mifs the favourable opportunity. I have many times found myfelf in that trying fituation.

What do you fay of this for example ? Day-light and powder were fpent one day in a Polifh foreft. When I was going home, a terrible bear made up to me in great fpeed, with open mouth, ready to fall upon me, all my pockets were fearched in an inftant for powder and ball, but in vain—I found nothing but two fpare flints ; one I flung with all my might into the monfter's open

jaws,

jaws, down his throat, It gave
him pain, and made him turn about,
so that I could level the second at
his back-door, which, indeed, I
did with wonderful success, for it
flew in, met the first flint in the
stomach, struck fire, and blew up
the bear with a terrible explosion.
Though I came safe off that time,
yet I should not wish to try it again,
or venture against bears with no
other defence.

There is a kind of fatality in it.
The fiercest and most dangerous
animals, generally come upon me
when defenceless, as if they had a
notion or foresight of it by way of
instinct,

inftinct. Thus a frightful wolf ruſhed upon me ſo ſuddenly, and ſo cloſe that I could do nothing but follow mechanical inftinct, and thruſt my fiſt into his open mouth. For ſafety's ſake I puſhed on, and on, till my arm was fairly in, up to the ſhoulder. 'How ſhould I diſengage myſelf?' I was not much pleaſed with my aukward ſituation—with a wolf face to face—our ogling was not of the moſt pleaſant kind. If I withdrew my arm, then the animal would fly the more furiouſly upon me; that, I ſaw in his flaming eyes. In ſhort, I laid hold of his intrails, turned him inſide out like

a glove,

a glove, and flung him to the ground, where I left him.

The same expedient would not have answered against a mad dog, which soon after came running against me in a narrow street at St. Petersburgh. Run who can, I thought; and the better to run I threw off my fur cloak, and was safe within doors in an instant. I sent my servant for the cloak, and he put it in the wardrobe with my other cloaths. The day after I was amazed and frightened by Jacks bawling: "For God's sake, Sir, your fur cloak is mad!" I hastened up to him, and found almost all

my

my cloaths toffed about and torn to
pieces. The fellow was perfectly
right in his apprehenfions about the
fur cloak's madnefs. I faw him
myfelf juft then falling upon a fine
full-drefs fuit, which he fhook and
toffed in an unmerciful manner.

All thefe narrow and lucky efcapes, Gentlemen, were chances
turned to advantage, by prefence of
mind and vigorous exertions; which
taken together, as every body knows,
makes the fortunate fportfman, fai-
lor and foldier; but he would be
a very blameable and imprudent
fportfman, admiral or general, who
would always depend upon chance

and

and his ftars, without troubling
himfelf about thofe arts which are
their particular purfuits, and without providing the very beft imple-
ments, which infure fuccefs. I was
not blameable either way; for I
have always been as remarkable for
the excellency of my horfes, dogs,
guns and fwords, as for the proper
manner of ufing and managing
them, fo that upon the whole I may
hope to be remembered in the foreft,
upon the turf, and in the field. I
fhall not enter here into any detail
of my ftables, kennel, or armoury,
but a favourite dog of mine I cannot
help mentioning to you. It was a
greyhound. I never had or faw a

better

better one. He grew old in my fervice, and was not remarkable for his
fize, but the rather for his uncom-
mon fwiftnefs. I always courfed with
him. Had you feen him, you muft
have admired him, and would not
have wondered at my predilection,
and at my courfing him fo much. He
run fo faft, fo much, and fo long in
my fervice, that he actually run off
his legs, fo that in the latter part of
his life, I was under the neceffity
of working and ufing him only as a
terrier, in which quality he ftill
ferved me many years.

Whilft a greyhound—I muft ob-
ferve fhe was a bitch—She courfed
one day a hare, which appeared to

D   me

me uncommonly big. I pitied my
poor bitch, fhe was big with pups,
yet fhe would courfe as faft as ever.
I could follow her on horfeback
only at a great diftance. At once
I heard a cry as it were of a pack of
hounds—but fo weak and faint,
that I hardly knew what to make
of it. Coming up at laft, I was
greatly furprifed. The hare had
littered in running; the fame had
happened to my bitch in courfing—
and there were juft as many leverets
as pups. By inftinct the former
run, the latter courfed, and thus, I
found myfelf in poffeffion at once
of fix hares, and as many dogs, at

the

the end of a course, which had only begun with one.

I remember this, my wonderful bitch, with the same pleasure and tenderness, as a superb Lithuanian horse, which no money could have bought. He became mine by an accident, which gave me an opportunity of shewing my horsemanship to a great advantage. I was at Count Przoboffky's noble country seat in Lithuania, and remained with the ladies at tea, in the drawing room, while the gentlemen were down in the yard, to see a young horse of blood, which was just arrived from the stud. At once we heard a noise

D 2   of

of diſtreſs—I haſtened down ſtairs,
and found the horſe ſo unruly that
nobody durſt approach or mount
him. The moſt reſolute horſemen
ſtood diſmayed and agaſt; deſpon-
dency was expreſſed in every coun-
tenance, when in one leap, I was
on his back, frightened him by
ſurprize, and worked him quite into
gentleneſs and obedience, with the
beſt diſplay of horſemanſhip I was
maſter of. Fully to ſhew this to
the ladies, and ſave them unneceſſary
trouble, I forced him to leap in at
one of the open windows of the tea
room, walked round ſeveral times,
pace, trot, and gallop; and at laſt
made him mount the tea-table, there

to

to repeat his leſſons, in a pretty ſtyle of miniature, which was exceedingly pleaſing to the ladies, for he performed them amazingly well, and did not break either cup or ſaucer. It put me ſo high in the opinion of the ladies, and ſo well in that of the noble lord, that with his uſual politeneſs he begged I would accept of this young horſe, and ride him full career to conqueſt and honor, in the campaign againſt the Turks, which was ſoon to be opened, under the command of Count Munich.

I could not indeed have received a more agreeable preſent, nor a more

ominous

omnious one at the opening of that
campaign, in which I made my
apprenticeship as a soldier. A horse
so gentle, so spirited, and so fierce
—at once a lamb and a Bucephalus,
put me always in mind of the soldier's and the gentleman's duty, of
young Alexander and of the asto-
nishing things he performed in the
field.

We took the field, among several other reasons it seems, with an
intention to retrieve the character
of the Russian arms, which had
been blemished a little by Czar
Peter's last campaign on the Pruth—
and this we fully accomplished by

several

feveral very fatiguing and glorious campaigns under the command of that great general I mentioned before.

Modefty forbids individuals, to arrogate to themfelves great fucceffes or victories, the glory of which is generally engroffed by the commander, nay, which is rather aukward, by kings and queens, who never fmelt gun-powder, but at the field days and reviews of their troops, never faw a field of battle or an enemy in battle array.

Not do I claim any particular fhare of glory in the great engage-

ments

ments with the enemy. We all
did our duty, which, in the patriots,
foldiers, and gentleman's language,
is a very comprehenfive word of
great honour, meaning and import,
and of which the generality of idle
quidnuncs and coffee-houfe politi-
cians, can hardly form any but a
very mean and contemptible idea.
However, having had the command
of a body of huzars, I have been on
feveral expeditions, with difcretion-
ary powers; and the fuccefs I then
met with, is, I think, fairly, and
only to be put to my account, and
to that of the brave fellows whom
I led to conqueft and to victory.
We had very hot work once in the

van

van of the army, when we drove the Turks into Oczackow. My spirited Lithuanian had almost brought me into a scrape. I had an advanced forepost, and saw the enemy coming against me in a cloud of dust, which left me rather uncertain about their actual numbers and real intentions. To wrap myself up in a similar cloud of dust was common prudence, but would not have much advanced my knowledge, or answered the end for which I had been sent out. Therefore I let my flankers on both wings spread to the right and left, and make what dust they could, and I myself led on straight upon the enemy.

my, to have a nearer fight of them; and that I had, gentlemen! for they ftood and fought, till for fear of my flankers, they began to move off rather diforderly. This was the moment to fall upon them with fpirit—We broke them entirely, made a terrible havock amongft them—and drove them not only back to a walled town in their rear, but even through it, contrary to our moft fanguine expectation.

By reafon of the fwiftnefs of my Lithuanian I had been foremoft in the purfuit; and feeing the enemy fairly flying through the oppofite gate, I thought it would be prudent

to

to ftop in the market-place to order
the trumpet to rendezvous. I ftopt,
gentlemen, but judge of my afton-
ifhment, when in this market-place
I faw neither trumpet nor any living
body of my huzars about me. Are
they fcouring the other ftreets? or
what is become of them? they could
not be far off, and muft, at all
events, foon join me. In that expectation I walked my panting Lithuanian to a fpring in the market-
place, and let him drink. He drunk
uncommonly—with an eagernefs
not to be fatisfied, but natural
enough, for when I looked round
for my men, what fhould I fee, gentlemen? the hind part of the poor
creature,

creature, croup and legs were miſ-
ſing, as if he had been cut in two,
and the water run out as it came in,
without either refreſhing him or
doing him any good. How it could
have happened was quite a miſtery
to me, till I returned with him to
the town gate. There I ſaw that
when I ruſhed in peace-meal with
the flying enemy, they had dropt the
port-cullis, and unperceived by me,
and the ſpirited animal, it had totally
cut off his hind part, which lay ſtill
quivering on the outſide of the gate.
It would have been an irreparable
loſs, had not our farrier contrived
to bring both parts together while
hot. He ſowed them up with
ſprigs

sprigs and young shoots of laurels that were just at hand—the wound healed and what could not have happened, but to so glorious a horse, the sprigs took root in his body, grew up, and formed a bower over me, so that afterwards I could go upon many other expeditions in the shade of my own and my horse's laurels.

But gentlemen, for all that; I was not always successful. I had even the misfortune to be overpowered by numbers, to be made prisoner of war; and what is worse, but always usual among the Turks, to be sold for a slave. In that state of

E   humiliation,

humiliation, my daily taſk was not
very hard, and laborious, but rather ſingular and irkſome. It was to
drive the Sultan's bees every morning to their paſture grounds, to at-
tend them all the day long and
againſt night to drive them back to
their hives. One evening I miſſed
a bee, and ſoon obſerved that two
bears had fallen upon her, to tear
her to pieces for the honey ſhe carried. I had nothing like an offen-
five weapon in my hands, but the
ſilver hatchet, which is the badge
of the Sultan's gardeners and far-
mers. I threw it at the robbers
with an intention to frighten them
away, and ſet the poor bee at liberty;
but

but by an unlucky turn of my arm, it flew upward—and flew, and flew, till it reached the moon. How fhould I recover it? How fetch it down again? I recollected that Turkey beans grew very quick, and run up to an aftonifhing height. I planted one immediately, it grew and actually faftened itfelf to one of the moon's horns. I had no more to do now, but to climb up by it into the moon, where I fafely arrived. I had a troublefome piece of work of it, before I could find my filver hatchet in a place where every thing has the brightnefs of filver. At laft however I found it in a heap of chaf and chopped ftraw.

E 2   I was

I was now for returning, but alas, the heat of the fun had dried up my bean; it was totally ufelefs for my defcent; fo I felt to work, and twifted me a rope of that chopped ftraw, as long and well as I could make it. This I faftened to one of the moon's horns, and flid down to the end of it. Here I held myfelf faft with the left hand, and with the hatchet in my right, I cut the long, now ufelefs end of the upper part, which when tied to the lower end brought me a good deal lower. However, this repeated fplicing and tying of the rope did not improve its quality nor bring me down to the Sultan's farms. I

was.

was ftill a couple of miles in the
clouds when it broke, and with
fuch violence I fell to the ground
that I found myfelf ftunned, and in
a hole nine fathoms under grafs,
when I recovered, hardly knowing
how to get out again. There was
no other way than to go home for
a fpade and to dig me out by flopes,
which I fortunately accomplifhed,
before I had been fo much as miffed
by the fteward.

Peace was foon after concluded
with the Turks, and it was favourable to Ruffia in fpite of French
politics. I recovered my liberty, and
left St. Peterfburgh at the time of

that

that fingular revolution about forty
years fince, when the emperor in
his cradle, his mother, the duke of
Brunfwick her father, field marfhal
Munich, and many others were fent
to Siberia. The winter was then
fo uncommonly fevere all over Europe, that ever fince the fun feems
to be froft-bitten—At my return to
this place, I felt on the road greater inconveniencies than thofe I had
experienced in my fetting out for
Ruffia. One effect of the froft
which I then obferved, is rather an
object for philofophical fpeculation.
I travelled poft day and night, and
finding myfelf engaged in a narrow
lane, I bid the poftilion give a fig-
nal

nal with his horn, that other tra-
vellers might not meet or ſtop
us in the narrow paſſage. He
blew with all his might, but all his
endeavours were in vain. He could
not make the horn ſpeak, which, as
he pretended to be a good performer,
was as unaccountable to him, as to
me, and rather unfortunately, for
ſoon after we found ourſelves in the
preſence of another coach coming
the other way. It was very trouble-
ſome for both parties in this horrid
weather, for there was no proceed-
ing either way, without taking the
carriages to pieces and putting them
together again, paſt each other. My
poor poſtilion and every body was
almoſt

almoſt froze to death. However
we reached the much-looked-for
ſtage, without further accident, and
well pleaſed and happy in our minds,
we all of us haſtened to warm and
refreſh ourſelves.

The poſtilion hung his great coat
and horn on a peg and ſate down
near the kitchen fire, to forget and
drown his cares. I ſat down on the
other ſide doing the ſame. Sudden-
ly we heard a *Tereng ! tereng, teng,
teng !* We looked round, and now
found the reaſon, why the poſtilion
had not been able to ſound his horn.
His tunes were frozen up in the
horn, and came out now by thawing,

ing, plain enough, and much to the credit of the driver, ſo that the honeſt fellow entertained us for ſome time with a variety of tunes, without putting his mouth to the horn. The king of Pruſſia's march —Over the hill and over the dale— An evening hymn, and many other favourite tunes came out, and the thawing entertainment concluded, as I ſhall this ſhort account of my Ruſſian travels with

God bleſs Great George our King.